66 Unrules to spark energy, courage, and conscious change

J.K. LLOYD
FROM THE AUTHOR OF *WHAT THE HELL NOW!?*

WHAT THE HELL NEXT!?

66

IGNITE POTENTIAL. REINVENT YOUR PATH.
IMPACT YOUR WORLD.

WHAT THE HELL NEXT!?

Now it's time to move—with purpose, with courage, with no apologies.

By J.K.Lloyd
Copyright © 2025 J.K.Lloyd

All rights reserved.
No part of this book may be reproduced or used in any manner without the express written permission of the author, except for the use of brief quotations in a book review or scholarly work.

For more information, please contact:
contact@whatthehellseries.com
whatthehellseries.com

Disclaimer:
The information contained in this book is for educational and informational purposes only and is not intended as medical or professional advice. The author and publisher disclaim any liability in connection with the use of this information.

About The Author
J.K. Lloyd
(MPrac NLP, Cert FT, Cert OD, Coaching)

Melbourne-born leadership and personal growth strategist, formally trained in NLP, organisational development, coaching and futurist thinking, who spent years bridging science, psychology, and philosophy into something most books forget - practical, human wisdom. Lloyd's work is fuelled by one core belief: we don't need more rules, we need courage to rewrite the ones holding us back.
Through The What The Hell Series, he helps people recalibrate their internal compass, rebuild confidence, and rediscover purpose, without apology, self-editing, or waiting until they're "more ready."
He works with leaders, parents, and everyday humans navigating their own "what the hell" moments, using a blend of neuroscience, narrative reframing, and pragmatic reflection.

BOOKS BY J.K. LLOYD

What The Hell Now!?
The perspective shift that helps you break patterns, rewire your mind, and own your story.

What The Hell Next!?
66 Unrules to spark energy, courage, and conscious change.

www.whatthehellseries.com | @whatthehellseries

Dedication

For the ones who refused to stay stuck.
For the ones who burned the map, not the dream.
And for the brave souls standing at the edge of *what the hell next?* — this one's for you.

"The next chapter isn't about becoming someone new — it's about remembering who you are and daring to live it, fully."

(— J.K. Lloyd, What The Hell Next!?)

Contents

Introduction - 9
How to Read This Book

Why Sixty-Six? - 10

How this book works - 10

The Origin of the Five Keys - 13
(A story about what holds us together and what sets us free.)

Understanding The Keys to Transformation - 14

Sixty-Six Unrules for life - 16 to 147

ENERGY - *The Spark to Begin*
Unrules that ignite purpose, action, and aliveness.
— The courage to start over
— Finding your why
— Letting go of the timeline
— Staying passionate without burning out

GROWTH - *The Stretch That Shapes You*
Unrules about change, learning, and becoming.
— Embracing discomfort
— Rewiring the brain through challenge
— Unlearning what no longer fits
— Turning small acts into transformation

REFLECTION - *The Mirror Within*
Unrules that invite awareness, self-honesty, and alignment.
— The permission to be fully you
— The paradoxical theory of change
— Listening to what your body knows
— Depth over noise

COURAGE - *The Leap Forward*
Unrules about action, rebellion, and creative risk.
— Living beyond the script
— Redefining success
— Setting boundaries
— Saying no like it's self-respect

EXPANSION - *The Infinite Game*
Unrules about connection, chaos, and meaning.
— Chaos as catalyst
— Reinventing your social life
— Leaving a legacy that lasts
— The freedom to begin again

The Final Word - 151
An Invitation to Keep Becoming

Notes & References - 153
The thinkers, scientists, and storytellers helped shape the ideas explored throughout What The Hell Next!?

Introduction: How to Read This Book

If you've read **What The Hell Now!?** you already know, this isn't your ordinary "self-help" book.
It's a living conversation between science, philosophy, and the messy, magnificent chaos of being human.

Neuroscience tells us our brains can rewire themselves through curiosity and discomfort.
Philosophy reminds us that meaning isn't handed to us — it's made, moment by moment.
And transformation? It's never a single leap. It's a thousand tiny rebellions of thought, habit, and choice.

This isn't a sequel. It's a continuation, a compass, a reference, a spark to keep you moving in whichever direction life points you next.
What The Hell Now!? helped you stop, reflect, and realign.
What The Hell Next!? is about motion, whether forward, sideways, diagonally, even upside down if that's where life takes you.
Because growth isn't a straight line.

"Life is a beautiful series of detours, collapses, and rebuilds that somehow get you exactly where you were meant to go all along."

Why Sixty-Six?

Because change takes time, about 66 days, to be precise.
Behavioural psychology and neuroscience research from University College London found that, on average, it takes 66 days to form a new habit, that is, to rewire your brain and make something new feel natural. Not 21, not overnight, but roughly two months of repetition, resistance, and recalibration.

That's what this book is: 66 ways to practice transformation.
Not rules to follow, but Unrules to live into.

You could read it in a day, sure. But if you take one Unrule a day and live with it — question it, try it, mess it up, return to it, by the end, you won't just have read a book. You'll have rewired the way you move through life, because growth isn't a single act of courage.
It's 66 quiet, brave repetitions of becoming.

How This Book Works

You don't read this book — you *wander* through it.
Pick it up, flip to any page, and land where you need to land.
There's no order, no rules, no pressure.

Each **Unrule** is a spark, an idea, a story, a reminder that you're still becoming.
Some will challenge you.
Some will soothe you.
Some might just make you laugh when you need it most.

Every Unrule is built around three things:

- **Reflection** – questions that nudge, not nag.
- **Experiment** – something small to try, not perfect.
- **Visual spark** – a line, symbol, or thought fragment that lingers in your mind long after you close the page.

You'll see patterns if you look closely, the echoes of chaos theory, brain science, philosophy, psychology, and raw human truth, but don't go looking for structure. Life isn't linear so why should this book be any different!

The Thread That Connects It All

Beneath all **66 Unrules** runs one idea:
You don't need fixing. You need remembering.

Each page invites you to peel back one more layer of who you've been told to be and rediscover what's real to you.
Your curiosity.
Your chaos.
Your courage.
Your connection.

These aren't lessons. They're liberations.
They don't tell you what to do; they remind you that you already know.

Before You Begin…

The Origin of the Five Keys

(A story about what holds us together and what sets us free.)

Before there were Unrules, there were keys. Not the kind that open doors, but the kind that unlock people. They weren't discovered all at once. They arrived slowly, one by one, during the messy middle of life. In burnout and breakthrough, heartbreak and laughter, each key showed up when one part of life cracked open and whispered, *look closer*.

The first was **Energy** — arriving in time on a morning when you almost gave up, but didn't. It taught that purpose isn't found, it's *fuelled* by curiosity, defiance, and aliveness.

The second was **Growth,** the quiet one that arrived after chaos. It showed that healing and learning are the same thing, and that every ending is just a seed disguised as loss.

The third key, **Reflection**, came like a mirror. It asked uncomfortable questions and held them without needing answers. It became the art of pausing, of listening between thoughts.

Then came **Courage**, unexpected and wild. It didn't knock. It kicked the door open. It reminded that risk is the only real teacher, and that creativity and fear often share the same heartbeat.

The final key, **Expansion**, arrived when everything felt connected, even amongst chaos. It taught that meaning isn't owned, it's shared. We don't just exist *in* the universe, we exist *with* it.

And so, these five keys became the rhythm of the work, the pulse behind every Unrule, every page, every question.

Five sparks to keep your human engine burning and five ways to come back to yourself.

Understanding The Keys:
Your Compass for the Unrules

Each Unrule in this book carries its own energy. It's a kind of emotional fingerprint.

You'll see a small Key at the end of every Unrule: a visual cue that represents its deeper pulse. These aren't just icons. They're reminders of what's being stirred, stretched, or reignited in you.

Think of them as your emotional compass: signals to guide how you read, reflect, and act.

Sometimes you'll meet a Key that feels bold and electric.
Other times, one that invites stillness or expansion.
There's no right one to chase as they all serve a purpose.
Let them speak to you.

How to Use the Keys:

When you finish an Unrule, pause for a second.
Ask yourself:

"What is this Key unlocking in me?"

You might find one keeps returning and that's not coincidence. That's the theme you're being invited to explore right now.

Your Compass for the Unrules

When you're ready…

Find a quiet corner.
Take a breath.
Let go of everything you think you "should" be doing.
Then open the book wherever your fingers land.
That's your message for today.
There's no right way to read this — only your way.
Because the only real rule here is simple:

There are no rules.
Just 66 Unrules … and the ones you'll write next.

Key	Theme	Represents
	Energy / Passion	The spark of courage, drive, and purpose — for Unrules about daring, doing, and following what lights you up.
	Growth / Renewal	The quiet evolution — for Unrules about healing, learning, and transformation.
	Reflection / Awareness	The inner mirror — for Unrules about mindfulness, self-understanding, and emotional clarity.
	Courage / Action	The ignition — for Unrules about momentum, bravery, and saying yes even when it's hard.
	Chaos / Expansion	The wild unknown — for Unrules about uncertainty, connection, and cosmic perspective.

UNRULE #1
The Courage to Start Over

Sometimes the hardest thing isn't beginning.
It's admitting you've outgrown what used to fit.

Maybe the job looks fine on paper, the relationship is "comfortable," the days blur in predictable loops — and yet something deep inside keeps whispering, *this isn't it.*

That whisper isn't restlessness. It's truth trying to surface.

Starting over isn't failure; it's evolution in motion. Nietzsche called it the *will to power* — the human pull to rise, to recreate, to become. Every time you shed an old version of yourself, you step closer to the one that can breathe again.

The real courage isn't leaping into the new.
It's standing in the doorway between what was and what could be, heart pounding, knowing you're about to rewrite the script.

Pause Here → Reflection

- Where in your life are you clinging to comfort disguised as stability?

- What part of you is whispering for change — and what would happen if you listened?

- If you weren't afraid of starting over, what would your next chapter look like?

Try This → Micro Experiment

Tonight, write a two-sentence "resignation letter" to the version of you that's done playing small.
Thank them for getting you this far.
Then sign your name, date it, and fold it into tomorrow's page.
Symbolic? Absolutely.
But your brain loves rituals — they mark beginnings.

Quick Wisdom Bite

"You are not starting from scratch.
You are starting from experience."

Key	Theme	Represents
⚡	Courage / Action	The ignition — for Unrules about momentum, bravery, and saying yes even when it's hard.

UNRULE #2
Live Beyond the Script

From the moment you could walk, someone handed you a script.
Be polite. Work hard. Don't make waves.
Follow the plan: study, earn, settle, retire, repeat.

And for a while, maybe you did. You played your role.
But one day, you catch yourself halfway through another polite conversation thinking, *Is this really mine?*

That's the moment the script starts to burn.

Living beyond it doesn't mean chaos for chaos' sake.
It means questioning what's been written for you — by family, by culture, by habit — and daring to ad-lib your own lines.

Nietzsche called this becoming the *Overman*: one who creates meaning instead of borrowing it.
It's less about rebellion and more about authorship.
You stop performing life and start directing it.

The trick? You don't have to throw out every scene.
Just rewrite the ones that no longer make sense.

Pause Here → Reflection
- Whose approval still shapes the choices you make?

- What rulebook are you still unconsciously following?

- If today were improv, what would you say or do differently?

Try This → Micro Experiment
Grab a notebook and title the page *The Rules I Never Agreed To*.
List every "should" that pops up — big or small.
Then, beside each one, write its opposite.
That second column?
That's where freedom lives.

Quick Wisdom Bite
"You don't have to burn the map.
Just stop pretending it's the only one."

Key	Theme	Represents
	Energy / Passion	The spark of courage, drive, and purpose — for Unrules about daring, doing, and following what lights you up.

UNRULE #3
The Permission to Be Fully You

You've spent years editing yourself — softening your edges, shrinking your volume, dressing your truth in something more "appropriate." Because somewhere along the line, someone made you believe that being too much was a flaw instead of a flame.

But the reality is: there is no medal for being digestible.

The world doesn't need another copy. It needs the unfiltered, unpolished, electric you.

Carl Rogers called it *congruence* — the alignment between who you are inside and how you show up outside.
When those two selves finally shake hands, something shifts.
Your nervous system exhales. Your relationships deepen. Life feels less like performance and more like belonging.

And yes, it's terrifying at first.
Because authenticity threatens every mask you've ever worn.
But the moment you stop apologising for your light, you'll realise it wasn't arrogance — it was aliveness.

Pause Here → Reflection

- Where are you still asking for permission to exist?

- What parts of yourself have you been editing out to fit in?

- What would your day look like if you stopped hiding?

Try This → Micro Experiment

Tomorrow, do one small thing that feels like *you* — unapologetically.
Wear the outfit. Share the idea. Say the thing you've been swallowing.
Notice how your body responds — lighter, louder, freer.
That's alignment speaking.

Quick Wisdom Bite

"Your real power doesn't come from fitting in.
It comes from no longer needing to."

Key	Theme	Represents
	Reflection / Awareness	The inner mirror — for Unrules about mindfulness, self-understanding, and emotional clarity.

UNRULE #4
Chaos Is the Catalyst

You don't have to have it all together.
In fact, trying to control every outcome is usually what keeps you stuck.

Change doesn't arrive in calm, symmetrical packages. It crashes through like a storm, flinging old certainties across the room.
And even as you curse the mess, some deeper part of you knows—this is the shake-up you needed.

Enter chaos theory: Edward Lorenz, 1960s mathematician, discovers that a butterfly flapping its wings in Brazil could set off a tornado in Texas.

Tiny disturbances. Huge consequences.
That's life. That's you.

One decision, one conversation, one "what the hell, let's try it" moment—and suddenly, the whole trajectory shifts.
Chaos isn't proof you've failed. It's proof you're alive.
It's the universe handing you a remix button.

Pause Here → Reflection

- Where is life currently refusing to follow your script?

- What are you trying to hold together that actually needs to fall apart?

- What if this disruption isn't punishment—but preparation?

Try This → Micro Experiment

Next time the day unravels—missed train, cancelled plans, curveball—pause and say out loud:
"Ah, the plot thickens."
Notice how that one line flips the mood from victim to co-author.
Then look for one opportunity the chaos created that didn't exist before.

Quick Wisdom Bite

"Chaos isn't the enemy of order.
It's the birthplace of transformation."

Key	Theme	Represents
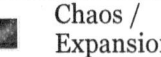	Chaos / Expansion	The wild unknown — for Unrules about uncertainty, connection, and cosmic perspective.

UNRULE #5
Embrace Discomfort Like a Training Ground

Your brain loves patterns.
Comfort zones. Predictable loops.
It calls them "safe," but what it really means is "unchallenged."

Growth doesn't happen in the comfy chair.
It happens in the stretch and in the awkward, sweaty, I-have-no-idea-what-I'm-doing spaces.

Neuroscience calls it neuroplasticity, your brain's ability to rewire itself through new experiences.

Every time you try something unfamiliar, struggle through it, and adapt, your neural pathways light up like fireworks.
That discomfort you feel? It's literally your brain growing.

Dr. Michael Merzenich proved it — adults can rewire their brains at any age. You can too. But only if you stop mistaking discomfort for danger. Because what if the unease you're avoiding isn't a red flag… but a green light?

Pause Here → Reflection
- What part of your life has become too predictable?

- When was the last time you felt both terrified and alive?

- What would you learn if you stopped resisting discomfort and leaned in?

Try This → Micro Experiment
Pick one thing you've been avoiding because it feels "too hard."
Do it badly.
Seriously — the goal isn't perfection, it's rewiring.
Each time you show up, your brain learns: *I can survive this.*
That's how resilience is built — not in theory, but in action.

Quick Wisdom Bite
"Discomfort isn't punishment.
It's your nervous system stretching into possibility."

Key	Theme	Represents
	Growth / Renewal	The quiet evolution — for Unrules about healing, learning, and transformation.

UNRULE #6
The Paradox of Change — Stop Forcing It

Sometimes the harder you chase transformation, the faster it runs from you.

You can't bully a butterfly out of its cocoon.
Carl Rogers called it the *Paradoxical Theory of Change*:
the moment you stop trying so hard to become something else — and instead accept where you are — the real change begins.

Acceptance doesn't mean giving up.

It means telling the truth about where you stand, without judgment.
Because until you see yourself clearly, you can't steer anywhere new.

Think of it like unclenching your fist.
The space you create by letting go is what allows new movement.
And yes, it's terrifying — to stop fixing, controlling, perfecting.
But transformation doesn't come from pushing harder;
it comes from finally exhaling.

Pause Here → Reflection

- What part of your life are you trying too hard to change?

- What would happen if you stopped forcing and started accepting?

- Where could honesty create more freedom than effort ever has?

Try This → Micro Experiment

For one week, stop self-improvement cold turkey.
No new hacks, no "better you" routines.
Instead, observe yourself with radical honesty.
Notice what changes naturally when you stop gripping so tightly.
That's the paradox: when you stop chasing growth, growth finds you.

Quick Wisdom Bite

"Change doesn't come from force.
It comes from finally allowing yourself to be real."

Key	Theme	Represents
	Reflection / Awareness	The inner mirror — for Unrules about mindfulness, self-understanding, and emotional clarity.

UNRULE #7
Reinvent Your Social Life

Let's be honest — most of us outgrow people long before we admit it. You keep meeting for coffee, smiling through small talk, pretending you still connect — but inside, it feels like static.

That's not failure.
It's evolution.

As you change, your social landscape should too.
Neuroscience says connection literally rewires the brain: oxytocin, dopamine, serotonin — the body's own alchemy for belonging.
But that chemistry only flows where there's truth.
Staying around people who drain you is like forcing your nervous system to run on fumes.

Real connection is energetic.
It's curiosity meeting curiosity, chaos meeting chaos.
When you find your people — the ones who see your weirdness as a feature, not a flaw — you don't just feel better, you think better.
Your brain lights up in empathy and creativity.

So, prune the noise.
Curate your circle.
Make space for the people who remind you that life is worth showing up for.

Pause Here → Reflection
- Who in your life leaves you lighter after being with them?

- Who leaves you smaller?

- What kind of people or communities could you invite in to reflect who you're becoming now?

Try This → Micro Experiment
For one week, treat your social life like spring cleaning.
Say *yes* only to the interactions that energise you.
Say *no* (politely) to the ones that drain you.
Notice what shifts — in mood, in focus, in how alive you feel.
That's your nervous system thanking you for recalibration.

Quick Wisdom Bite
"The company you keep isn't just shaping your calendar —
it's shaping your chemistry."

Key	Theme	Represents
	Growth / Renewal	The quiet evolution — for Unrules about healing, learning, and transformation.

UNRULE #8
Be the Observer, Not the Judge

Your mind loves to narrate.
It's constantly sorting, labelling, predicting — a commentary track that never shuts up. Good, bad. Right, wrong. Success, failure.

But here's the twist: most of what it's judging isn't reality — it's memory dressed up as truth.

Neuroscience calls this predictive coding: your brain doesn't perceive the world as it is, but as it *expects* it to be.
You're not reacting to the present moment — you're reacting to your past conditioning about the present moment.
And that's why so many of us feel stuck. We're living inside recycled judgments, mistaking them for clarity.

Observation is the antidote.

When you step back and witness your thoughts without trying to fix them, something miraculous happens. The storm of self-criticism loses power. You stop fighting shadows. You see patterns instead of problems.

Carl Jung called this *holding the tension of opposites* — the courage to see both light and shadow without collapsing into either.
Observation doesn't mean passivity; it means presence.
You become the calm eye of your own hurricane.
And the paradox?
When you stop judging what *is*, you create space for change to *become*.

Pause Here → Reflection

- What thoughts replay most often — and what emotion are they really protecting?

- When you observe without fixing, what happens to your energy?

- Can you name one area of your life that needs less judgment and more witnessing?

Try This → Micro Experiment

For one day, treat your thoughts like passing weather.
Each time one drifts in, label it neutrally — *"thinking," "remembering," "worrying."*
Then let it float on.
By day's end, notice which thoughts lost their grip when you simply watched them go.

Quick Wisdom Bite

"You don't need to silence the mind.
You just need to stop believing everything it says."

Key	Theme	Represents
	Reflection / Awareness	The inner mirror — for Unrules about mindfulness, self-understanding, and emotional clarity.

UNRULE #9
Stop Waiting for Confidence

Somewhere along the line, you were told confidence is the ticket — the magical feeling that arrives first, makes you ready, and then you act. But neuroscience says otherwise. Confidence doesn't precede action; it follows it. It's built molecule by molecule through repetition, failure, and survival.

The prefrontal cortex, the part of your brain that deals with planning and fear regulation, doesn't fully switch on until you do something. Until you take the step, make the call, hit "publish," or speak up in the room. Every time you move despite fear, your brain releases a small reward — dopamine, serotonin, the quiet chemistry of courage. Action tells your system: We're safe. We can do this again.

Most people wait for a day that never comes — the day they'll "feel ready."

Readiness isn't a feeling. It's a decision. You don't need the full plan.

You just need to shift the weight of your body from hesitation to momentum.

Confidence isn't loud or polished; it's a quiet agreement with yourself to keep showing up. Every stumble, every awkward first attempt is confidence in its rawest form: proof that you're moving.

Pause Here → Reflection

- What dream or change have you kept parked in "someday"?

- What story are you telling yourself about why you're not ready yet?

- What would happen if you replaced "ready" with "willing"?

Try This → Micro Experiment

Pick one thing you've been circling — that call, application, or post.
Do it *today*, before you have time to talk yourself out of it.
Then record how your body feels afterward — lighter, electric, alive.
That's your nervous system memorising courage.

Quick Wisdom Bite

"You don't become confident by waiting.
You become confident by moving scared until you don't have to."

Key	Theme	Represents
⚡	Courage / Action	The ignition — for Unrules about momentum, bravery, and saying yes even when it's hard.

UNRULE #10
Doubt Means You're in Motion

If you feel unsure, restless, or full of questions — good. It means you're not sleepwalking anymore. Doubt is the bruise that proves you're leaning into life. It shows up whenever you leave the familiar edges of what you know.

Philosophers and scientists alike have celebrated doubt as a catalyst for growth. René Descartes began his entire philosophy with "I doubt, therefore I think." Psychologist Abraham Maslow suggested that uncertainty is the birthplace of self-actualisation — that the most fulfilled humans are not the ones who *know*, but the ones who *wonder*.

We tend to treat doubt like a virus to eradicate. But it's a signal — a flashing light saying: *Here lies potential.*

Certainty is static; doubt is dynamic. It's the space between what you were and what you're becoming.

If you're doubting the job, the relationship, the direction — it's not failure. It's your inner compass recalibrating. Let it. Doubt means you've grown too big for the old container.

Pause Here → Reflection

- What part of your life has started to feel too small?

- Where is doubt pointing you toward expansion rather than retreat?

- What would happen if you thanked uncertainty instead of fighting it?

Try This → Micro Experiment

For one week, every time self-doubt whispers, write down its message.

Then answer it with curiosity: *What is this teaching me about what I want next?*

You'll notice your fear slowly turning into fuel.

Quick Wisdom Bite

"Doubt isn't weakness.

It's your mind stretching toward a bigger truth."

Key	Theme	Represents
	Reflection / Awareness	The inner mirror — for Unrules about mindfulness, self-understanding, and emotional clarity.

UNRULE #11
Turn Comparison Into Calibration

(Use Envy as Information)

Comparison is one of the most misunderstood emotions. We shame ourselves for it, pretending not to care while secretly scrolling through someone else's highlight reel. But envy, when looked at closely, isn't evil — it's intel. It reveals what you value but haven't yet claimed.

Envy is inviting you to notice what in you is ready to awaken.

Neuroscientists found that the brain lights up in the same regions when we experience envy and when we feel motivation. The difference is interpretation. You can use that energy to punish yourself — or to propel yourself.

When you see someone thriving, ask: *What part of this reflects something I secretly want?* Maybe it's not their job or partner — maybe it's their freedom, their creativity, their courage. Envy isn't telling you to copy them; it's inviting you to notice what in you is ready to awaken. Reframed this way, comparison becomes calibration — a subtle compass aligning you closer to your authentic path.

Pause Here → Reflection

- Who triggers your comparison reflex the most — and why?

- What might their life be mirroring back about your next step?

- How can you use that spark as a signpost rather than a weapon?

Try This → Micro Experiment

Next time envy hits, write: *What does this person's story activate in me?*
Translate that emotion into one small, inspired action toward your own desire.

Quick Wisdom Bite

"Comparison isn't poison.
It's the universe whispering, 'You want that kind of aliveness too.'"

Key	Theme	Represents
	Growth / Renewal	The quiet evolution — for Unrules about healing, learning, and transformation.

UNRULE #12
Redefine Failure as Feedback

Failure isn't a dead end. It's data. Every misstep, rejection, or collapse is your nervous system learning new choreography.

Neuroscience calls this *error-based learning*. Your brain strengthens its neural pathways more effectively through mistakes than through perfection. Each time you fall and recalibrate, your system builds resilience, literally remapping the circuitry of success.

The people you admire most didn't avoid failure. They cultivated intimacy with it. They learned to fail forward — quicker, cleaner, kinder.

Failure isn't proof you're off path; it's the feedback that tells you you're still moving.

Thomas Edison reframed his "10,000 failed attempts" as 10,000 lessons in illumination. Michael Jordan said he succeeded because of his missed shots, not in spite of them.

You're not meant to get it right every time. You're meant to *stay in the arena* long enough to learn.

Pause Here → Reflection

- What are you calling failure that might actually be training?

- What story would you tell if you saw your mistakes as experiments?

- How might compassion accelerate your learning curve?

Try This → Micro Experiment

Pick one "failure" from your past and rewrite it as a research note. Name what it taught you, and how it strengthened you.
This simple reframing literally retrains your memory network from shame to growth.

Quick Wisdom Bite

"You're not failing — you're collecting data for your future brilliance."

Key	Theme	Represents
	Reflection / Awareness	The inner mirror — for Unrules about mindfulness, self-understanding, and emotional clarity.

UNRULE #13
Let Curiosity Lead

Curiosity is one of humanity's oldest survival instincts. It got our ancestors out of caves, across oceans, and into new ideas. Yet as adults, we often trade wonder for control. We stop exploring and start managing.

When you follow what fascinates you — even slightly — your brain's reward system lights up. Dopamine fires not when you *find* answers, but when you *seek* them. That means curiosity literally propels you forward; it's nature's way of turning fear into forward motion.

Fear shrinks your world. Curiosity expands it.

Every "What if?" you chase stretches your neural network, builds resilience, and reconnects you with creativity — that childlike spark that hasn't left you, just been buried under to-do lists and expectations.

You don't need to know where curiosity will take you. You just need to follow the thread. Sometimes it leads to passion, sometimes to purpose, sometimes to a complete plot twist. All of them count.

Pause Here → Reflection
- What topic, place, or idea quietly tugs at your attention lately?

- When did you last let yourself learn purely for the joy of it?

- What might happen if you followed fascination more than fear this month?

Try This → Micro Experiment
Every morning for one week, ask yourself: *What am I curious about today?*
Then, dedicate ten minutes to exploring it — a video, a book, a question, a walk.
You're training your brain to replace anxiety with wonder.

Quick Wisdom Bite
"When fear whispers 'what if it goes wrong,'
curiosity replies, 'what if it goes somewhere extraordinary?'"

Key	Theme	Represents
🔥	Energy / Passion	The spark of courage, drive, and purpose — for Unrules about daring, doing, and following what lights you up.

UNRULE #14
Stop Outsourcing Your Worth

At some point, most of us were trained to chase gold stars — the teacher's praise, the boss's nod, the hearts and likes on screens. We built our sense of self like a stock price: fluctuating wildly based on outside reactions.

But here's the fact: external validation is a loan with cruel interest. The more you depend on it, the further you drift from your own centre.

Validation Is Not a Renewable Resource.

Neuroscientists call this the *social approval loop* — dopamine spikes when others approve of you, but the crash that follows makes you crave the next fix. It's not self-esteem; it's chemical dependency dressed as popularity.

True worth isn't something you earn. It's something you reclaim. The moment you stop performing for applause, you start operating from integrity. When you anchor your value internally, you become steady — no longer blown about by other people's weather systems.

Self-validation isn't arrogance. It's emotional maturity. It's saying: *I like who I am when nobody's watching.*

Pause Here → Reflection

- Whose approval do you still quietly crave?

- How often do you measure your worth through someone else's reaction?

- What would your day feel like if you decided you were already enough?

Try This → Micro Experiment

Each morning, look in the mirror and name one thing you appreciate about yourself — something internal, not aesthetic.
Repeat it aloud until it lands. You're rewiring the voice of authority from external to internal.

Quick Wisdom Bite

"Validation borrowed is validation lost.
Respect yourself first — applause is optional."

Key	Theme	Represents
	Reflection / Awareness	The inner mirror — for Unrules about mindfulness, self-understanding, and emotional clarity.

UNRULE #15
Play Your Way Forward

Remember when life felt like an experiment — mud pies, dance floors, imagination at full volume? Somewhere along the way, adulthood traded play for productivity. But play isn't the opposite of work — it's the fuel of creativity.

Research from the University of Pennsylvania shows that adults who integrate playful exploration into problem-solving outperform those who grind relentlessly. Play expands cognitive flexibility, strengthens emotional regulation, and ignites innovative thinking.

Serious Isn't the Same as Significant.

When you allow yourself to play — to paint badly, cook chaotically, invent, build, or dance — your brain shifts from stress to flow. The prefrontal cortex relaxes; insight sneaks in.

Play is not childish; it's genius unchained.
Life's most significant leaps rarely come from whiteboards. They come from curiosity meeting joy.

Pause Here → Reflection

- Where have you equated seriousness with importance?

- When was the last time you lost track of time because you were having fun?

- What might "play" look like in your world now?

Try This → Micro Experiment

Schedule one playful hour this week — paint, dance, build, create, laugh.
Notice how your energy resets and your ideas multiply.
That's not indulgence — it's neurochemical innovation.

Quick Wisdom Bite

"Play doesn't distract you from your purpose.
It reminds you of it."

Key	Theme	Represents
	Energy / Passion	The spark of courage, drive, and purpose — for Unrules about daring, doing, and following what lights you up.

UNRULE #16

Let Rest Be Radical

We've glorified exhaustion like it's a badge of honour. "Busy" became the default response to "How are you?" — as if rest were rebellion. But your brain is not a machine; it's an ecosystem. It needs seasons, cycles, and stillness to stay alive.

When you rest, your *glymphatic system* goes to work — flushing toxins, consolidating memories, and integrating learning. Without it, burnout isn't a risk; it's inevitable.

Doing Nothing Is Still Doing Something.

Neuroscientist Andrew Huberman calls rest "active recovery." It's when your brain rewires everything you've learned. So yes, that nap, that quiet walk, that Netflix hour — it's part of your creative process, not an interruption of it.

Rest is radical in a culture addicted to productivity. It's a declaration that your worth isn't measured in output. That you can pause without losing momentum, because recovery is where energy is reborn.

Pause Here → Reflection
- What belief makes you feel guilty about resting?

- How do you know when your body is asking for stillness?

- What kind of rest actually refuels you — solitude, nature, sleep, laughter?

Try This → Micro Experiment
Block out rest in your calendar *before* adding work tasks.
Guard it like a meeting with your future self.
Observe how your creativity and clarity rebound.

Quick Wisdom Bite
"Rest isn't retreat.
It's where the next chapter gathers strength."

Key	Theme	Represents
	Growth / Renewal	The quiet evolution — for Unrules about healing, learning, and transformation.

UNRULE #17

Make Peace with the Mess

We crave tidy arcs — clean lines, predictable outcomes, polished lives. But real progress looks like chaos in motion. Mess is movement wearing its work clothes.

In nature, growth is never symmetrical. Forests regenerate through decay. Rivers change shape through erosion. Even stars are born from cosmic dust. Your evolution will be just as unruly — scribbles, revisions, false starts.

Progress Has Fingerprints All Over It.

The pursuit of perfection is a fear response. It's control disguised as discipline. When you accept the mess as proof that you're experimenting, you shift from judgment to curiosity. The question stops being "Why am I not there yet?" and becomes "What am I learning here?"

Progress is not a straight line — it's a heartbeat. Spikes, dips, pauses, rhythm. Mess means you're alive.

Pause Here → Reflection

- What parts of your life look chaotic right now?

- What story are you telling about that chaos?

- How could you reframe it as evidence of transformation?

Try This → Micro Experiment

Leave one task, project, or room imperfect this week — intentionally.
Resist the urge to fix it.
Notice how your nervous system reacts and then relaxes.

Quick Wisdom Bite

"Mess is not the enemy of mastery.
It's the workshop where mastery is made."

Key	Theme	Represents
⚡	Courage / Action	The ignition — for Unrules about momentum, bravery, and saying yes even when it's hard.

UNRULE #18
Turn Fear into Fuel

Your body doesn't know the difference between fear and excitement — chemically, they're identical. The same adrenaline that floods you before a presentation is what races through your veins before a first kiss. The label you give it defines your experience.

Next time your heart pounds, don't rush to calm it — reframe it. Say: *"This is energy. This means I care."* Fear isn't a sign you're on the wrong path. It's proof you're close to something meaningful.

Adrenaline Is Just Excitement in Costume.

Adventurers, athletes, performers — they all feel fear. The difference? They've learned to ride it instead of resist it. Over time, the brain learns that high arousal doesn't equal danger — it equals readiness.

Fear, reframed, becomes fuel. It sharpens your senses, anchors your focus, and signals that you're alive at the edge of your potential.

Pause Here → Reflection

- Where does fear show up most for you — and what dream is hiding behind it?

- What's the story you tell yourself when fear arrives?

- How could you reinterpret that rush as momentum instead of threat?

Try This → Micro Experiment
Before your next high-stakes moment, whisper: *"Same chemicals, different story."*
Then breathe deeply and lean in.
Notice how fear transforms into electricity.

Quick Wisdom Bite
"Fear is the body's way of saying:
'You're on the verge of expansion.'"

Key	Theme	Represents
⚡	Courage / Action	The ignition — for Unrules about momentum, bravery, and saying yes even when it's hard.

UNRULE #19
Let Go of Linear

We've been sold a myth: that life moves in clean upward graphs — always improving, always advancing. But nature laughs at linear. Trees lose leaves to prepare for spring. Tides retreat before they surge. You, too, have seasons.

Growth is cyclical — expansion, contraction, rest, renewal. Expecting endless upward momentum only breeds exhaustion. Neuroscience shows that consolidation — the quiet phase after learning — is where the brain strengthens new pathways. That plateau you hate? It's not stagnation. It's cementing progress.

Growth Has Seasons, Not Schedules.

Once you stop demanding constant bloom, you begin to trust the rhythm of becoming. There will be winters of reflection, summers of expansion, autumns of letting go — all vital, all temporary.

You're not behind. You're in season.

Pause Here → Reflection

- What season are you in right now — planting, blooming, shedding, or resting?

- How do you treat yourself when you're not "producing"?

- What wisdom might be growing quietly beneath the surface?

Try This → Micro Experiment

Track your energy instead of your achievements for one month.
Watch the patterns emerge.
Then align your effort with your energy, not against it.

Quick Wisdom Bite

"Linear is for machines.
You're made of cycles, seasons, and rhythm."

Key	Theme	Represents
🌿	Growth / Renewal	The quiet evolution — for Unrules about healing, learning, and transformation.

UNRULE #20
Rewrite the Definition of Success

Success used to mean climbing ladders, collecting titles, ticking boxes. But that script often ends in burnout. You know, the quiet ache of "I made it... but I'm still not happy."

Real success isn't about scale. It's about *sensation,* that felt sense of alignment between what you do and who you are. Fulfilment is measurable only from the inside out.

Psychologist Mihaly Csikszentmihalyi described flow as the state where challenge meets meaning, not comfort, not chaos, but purpose in motion. That's success: when your days stretch you just enough to make you proud without leaving you empty.

Fulfilment Over Finish Lines.

So redefine it. Success could mean being kind under pressure, or creating art no one else sees. It could mean peace over prestige. When your metrics change, your life expands.

Pause Here → Reflection
- Whose definition of success are you still performing for?

- What would success feel like — not look like — in your body?

- What might change if you valued fulfilment over recognition?

Try This → Micro Experiment
Write a new success statement:
"I'll know I'm successful when I feel ____."
Keep it visible. Let it guide your decisions for one week.

Quick Wisdom Bite
"Success isn't louder.
It's truer."

Key	Theme	Represents
	Reflection / Awareness	The inner mirror — for Unrules about mindfulness, self-understanding, and emotional clarity.

UNRULE #21
Master the Micro Shift

Transformation rarely arrives in grand gestures. It hides in small, repeated acts, the micro shifts you almost dismiss. Neuroscientists call this "habit stacking" , those tiny, consistent adjustments that rewire your neural networks far faster than one-off revolutions.

The brain's *basal ganglia* loves efficiency. It turns new choices into autopilot through repetition, not intensity. So the goal isn't radical overhaul — it's gentle persistence. One walk. One brave email. One minute of meditation. Do it enough times and your brain believes: *This is who we are now.*

Small Changes. Massive Momentum.

Micro shifts compound. James Clear called it the "1% rule" — improve something by 1% daily, and within months your life looks unrecognisable.

You don't need a new identity overnight; you need a series of nudges that slowly evolve your nervous system toward possibility.

Pause Here → Reflection

- What's one micro habit you could start today that aligns with your future self?

- What small decision could you repeat daily that would build trust with yourself?

- Where are you confusing "slow" with "stuck"?

Try This → Micro Experiment

Choose one behaviour that feels doable — a daily walk, journaling three lines, a gratitude check.
Do it for seven days. Track not the result, but the identity shift: *I'm someone who shows up.*

Quick Wisdom Bite

"Big change isn't dramatic.
It's microscopic — repeated until it becomes muscle memory."

Key	Theme	Represents
	Growth / Renewal	The quiet evolution — for Unrules about healing, learning, and transformation.

UNRULE #22
Emotions Are Messengers, Not Enemies

Most of us were taught to manage emotions by avoiding them. "Be strong." "Stay positive." "Don't cry." But neuroscience tells a different story: suppressed emotions don't disappear — they reroute.

Research from UCLA shows that simply naming an emotion reduces amygdala activity (the brain's threat centre) by up to 40%.
In other words, awareness disarms chaos.
Feeling doesn't make you weak. It makes you integrated.

Feel It. Don't Become It.

Emotions are messengers, not verdicts. Anger points to violated boundaries. Sadness signals loss or disconnection. Anxiety highlights uncertainty that needs compassion, not control. When you listen without judgement, emotions become data — the nervous system's way of saying, "Pay attention here."

The goal isn't to fix feelings. It's to metabolise them — to let them move through you without building a permanent home.

Pause Here → Reflection
- Which emotions do you judge or suppress most often?

- What messages might they be trying to deliver?

- How would it feel to name your emotion out loud instead of hiding it?

Try This → Micro Experiment
Next time you feel something strong, label it: "This is fear," or "This is grief."
Then ask, "What do you need?"
You're teaching your brain that emotions are signals, not threats.

Quick Wisdom Bite
"Emotions don't derail you.
Ignoring them does."

Key	Theme	Represents
	Reflection / Awareness	The inner mirror — for Unrules about mindfulness, self-understanding, and emotional clarity.

UNRULE #23
Build Friction into the Right Places

Your environment is shaping you, silently, constantly. Behavioural science shows that 80% of your daily decisions aren't conscious choices but environmental defaults. The cue, not the willpower, wins.

Want to exercise more? Put the shoes by the door.
Want to scroll less? Delete the app.
Want to write more? Open the document first thing.

Make the Good Easy and the Numbing Hard.

You don't rise to the level of your goals. You fall to the level of your systems. By adding friction to the habits that drain you and removing friction from the ones that fuel you, you architect your behaviour.

Friction is not resistance; it's direction.

Pause Here → Reflection
- What behaviours feel out of alignment with who you want to be?

- What cues in your environment reinforce them?

- Where could you swap friction and flow to serve your goals?

Try This → Micro Experiment
Pick one habit you want to amplify.
Ask: How can I make this easier to start?
Then choose one habit to reduce and ask: How can I make this slightly harder to access?
You've just hacked your autopilot.

Quick Wisdom Bite
"You don't need more motivation.
You need better architecture."

Key	Theme	Represents
⚡	Courage / Action	The ignition — for Unrules about momentum, bravery, and saying yes even when it's hard.

UNRULE #24
Your Body Keeps the Score — So Listen

You can think your way through almost anything — until your body calls your bluff.

Stress, anxiety, burnout, resentment — they don't vanish because you rationalise them. They surface as headaches, fatigue, tight chests, and restless sleep.

Somatic psychology calls this "embodied memory." Your body stores what your mind avoids. But the reverse is also true: your body can heal what your mind can't.

Movement, breathwork, laughter, dance — all signal to your nervous system that it's safe to release.

Wisdom Lives Below the Neck.

If the mind is the narrator, the body is the truth-teller. When you start listening to its language — tension, posture, gut instincts — you reclaim an entire dimension of intelligence you were trained to ignore.

Pause Here → Reflection

- What physical sensations show up when you're stressed or disconnected?

- How does your body tell you the truth before your mind admits it?

- What movement feels like medicine to you?

Try This → Micro Experiment

Once a day, pause and scan your body from head to toe.
Where's the tension? Name it.
Then take three slow breaths into that space.
Release — not through force, but awareness.

Quick Wisdom Bite

"The mind narrates stories.
The body speaks in truths."

Key	Theme	Represents
	Reflection / Awareness	The inner mirror — for Unrules about mindfulness, self-understanding, and emotional clarity.

UNRULE #25
Train Your Brain Like It's a Muscle

Your brain is not static hardware — it's adaptable, electric, constantly rewiring based on use. Neuroscientists call this *neuroplasticity*. Every time you learn, practice, or repeat a behaviour, your neural connections strengthen like fibers after a workout.

Dr. Michael Merzenich proved that even damaged brains can rebuild networks through focused repetition. Learning is physical — dendrites growing, synapses firing, new highways forming in grey matter.

That means every skill you admire — empathy, resilience, creativity — is trainable.

You're not "bad at it." You're just under-rehearsed.

Stop treating growth like a personality trait and start treating it like a gym membership. You don't need innate talent — just deliberate reps.

Pause Here → Reflection
- What skill or quality do you wish came "naturally" to you?

- What would it look like to train it instead of wish for it?

- How might consistency become your new superpower?

Try This → Micro Experiment
Identify one strength you'd like to build — patience, focus, creativity.
Practice it daily for 10 minutes.
Track not your perfection but your persistence.

Quick Wisdom Bite
"You're not stuck.
You're just undertrained."

Key	Theme	Represents
🌿	Growth / Renewal	The quiet evolution — for Unrules about healing, learning, and transformation.

UNRULE #26
Confidence Is Just Remembered Evidence

We often think of confidence as an emotion — something we summon when needed. But it's actually a memory system. Confidence is the brain recalling past evidence that you can handle uncertainty.

Each time you survive discomfort, deliver under pressure, or make it through something you thought you couldn't, your hippocampus stores that as *proof*. Later, when fear rises, **confidence is just your mind replaying those highlight reels.**

So when you feel low on self-belief, don't try to inflate your ego — go data mining. Pull up the receipts of resilience. Confidence isn't built in the mirror; it's built in motion, archived in the nervous system.

Pause Here → Reflection

- When was the last time you surprised yourself with your own strength?

- What evidence of capability are you forgetting to count?

- How can you catalogue your courage for next time?

Try This → Micro Experiment

Create a "Proof of Power" list — five times you did something hard.
Keep it somewhere visible.
Next time fear whispers, read it aloud.

Quick Wisdom Bite

"Confidence isn't found.
It's remembered."

Key	Theme	Represents
⚡	Courage / Action	The ignition — for Unrules about momentum, bravery, and saying yes even when it's hard.

UNRULE #27
You Can't Heal in a Hurry

Healing, whether emotional, mental, or physical — refuses to follow a timeline. It's not a sprint; it's seasonal. The nervous system heals through repetition, not rush.

When you pressure yourself to "get over it," you're activating the same stress chemistry that caused the wound.

Pace Is Part of the Process.

Research in trauma therapy (Dr. Peter Levine's *Waking the Tiger*) shows that repair happens through rhythm — slow release, re-sensation, rest. The brain and body relearn safety inch by inch.

So stop measuring recovery by speed. Measure it by softness. If today you can breathe easier, that's progress. If you can laugh again, that's a miracle.

Healing is not linear, but it's loyal and it always answers patience.

Pause Here → Reflection
- Where are you rushing your own recovery?

- What does "slow healing" look like in your life right now?

- How would your body feel if you trusted time?

Try This → Micro Experiment
For one week, replace "What's wrong with me?" with "What's still mending?"
Notice how compassion slows the panic and speeds the peace.

Quick Wisdom Bite
"Healing doesn't respond to deadlines.
It responds to devotion."

Key	Theme	Represents
	Growth / Renewal	The quiet evolution — for Unrules about healing, learning, and transformation.

UNRULE #28
Resilience Isn't Toughness — It's Flexibility

We glorify toughness — grit your teeth, push through, never falter. But resilience isn't rigidity; it's adaptability.

Biologically, resilience is the nervous system's ability to return to baseline after stress. The more flexible your system, the faster you recover.

Bend So You Don't Break.

Trees survive storms not because they resist wind, but because they bend with it. The same applies to you. Flexibility , whether mental, emotional, physical, is the quiet strength that outlasts force.

Resilience doesn't roar. It breathes.

Pause Here → Reflection

- What does resilience look like for you — endurance or elasticity?

- How do you currently recover from stress?

- What practices help you bend without breaking?

Try This → Micro Experiment

Start a "reset ritual" after tough days — breath, music, stretch, journal.
Train your body to return to calm faster each time.
You're building emotional elasticity.

Quick Wisdom Bite

"Real strength isn't how hard you hit.
It's how softly you can return."

Key	Theme	Represents
	Growth / Renewal	The quiet evolution — for Unrules about healing, learning, and transformation.

UNRULE #29
Repetition Is the Real Ritual

We tend to romanticise transformation, that spark, the breakthrough, the lightning-bolt moment. But real change doesn't come from epiphanies. It comes from repetition — showing up, even when it's boring, even when no one's watching.

Every repeated act strengthens your neural pathways like a groove deepening in stone. Neuroscience calls it *long-term potentiation* — neurons that fire together wire together. Each repetition tells your brain: *This matters. Keep it.*

Discipline Is Devotion in Disguise.

That's why rituals matter more than resolutions. A ritual isn't discipline for its own sake; it's a sacred vote for who you're becoming.

Repetition isn't punishment. It's proof of commitment.

Pause Here → Reflection
- What actions could become rituals of becoming for you?

- Where have you mistaken boredom for failure?

- How would it feel to see consistency as reverence?

Try This → Micro Experiment
Choose one small action you can ritualise — journaling, stretching, gratitude, reflection.
Do it at the same time for seven days.
Don't chase results. Chase rhythm.

Quick Wisdom Bite
"Discipline isn't dull.
It's how devotion becomes visible."

Key	Theme	Represents
	Growth / Renewal	The quiet evolution — for Unrules about healing, learning, and transformation.

UNRULE #30
Stop Negotiating with Procrastination

You're not lazy. You're protecting yourself.
Procrastination isn't a moral flaw; it's a nervous-system defence. When your brain senses a task linked to stress, shame, or uncertainty, it triggers avoidance — a biological attempt to keep you safe from failure.

Researchers at Harvard found that procrastinators experience higher activity in the *amygdala* — the threat centre of the brain. The task itself isn't scary; what it represents is. Perfectionism, fear of judgment, fear of change — all hide beneath the delay.

It's Not Laziness — It's Protection.

The trick isn't fighting procrastination. It's soothing it.
Break the task into micro steps, lower the threat, and your brain reclassifies it as safe. Suddenly, momentum returns.

Pause Here → Reflection

- What fear hides behind your most persistent procrastination?

- What emotion are you avoiding when you delay?

- How can you make the next step feel safe enough to start?

Try This → Micro Experiment

When you catch yourself avoiding, pause and say: *"I'm not lazy. I'm anxious."*
Take one five-minute action toward the task — timer on, pressure off. Progress will follow peace.

Quick Wisdom Bite

"Procrastination isn't disobedience.
It's your nervous system asking for reassurance."

Key	Theme	Represents
	Reflection / Awareness	The inner mirror — for Unrules about mindfulness, self-understanding, and emotional clarity.

UNRULE #31
Let Curiosity Outrun Perfectionism

Perfectionism is fear wearing ambition's clothes. It whispers, *"Don't start until it's flawless."* Curiosity says, *"Start — and see what happens."*

When you let curiosity take the lead, you bypass the brain's perfection loop. Dopamine, the motivation chemical, activates at the start of a quest, not at the finish line. That means your biology rewards movement, not mastery.

Start Before You're Ready — Stay Because You're Curious.

Curiosity is both antidote and engine. It doesn't need guarantees; it just needs permission.

Pause Here → Reflection
- Where are you waiting for permission to begin?

- What would change if progress mattered more than polish?

- How can curiosity make the process more playful?

Try This → Micro Experiment
Start something imperfect — write, paint, record, apply.
When perfectionism interrupts, say: *"I'm just exploring."*
Your nervous system relaxes when you frame effort as experiment.

Quick Wisdom Bite
"Curiosity creates.
Perfectionism procrastinates."

Key	Theme	Represents
	Energy / Passion	The spark of courage, drive, and purpose — for Unrules about daring, doing, and following what lights you up.

UNRULE #32
Anchor Yourself in the Present Moment

Anxiety lives in the future; regret lives in the past. Presence is the only place peace can visit.

Mindfulness isn't about lotus positions or empty minds — it's about returning to *now*, again and again, until it becomes home.

The brain loves to time travel, but the body only exists here. When you anchor through your senses — breath, texture, sound — your nervous system recalibrates. The *default mode network*, responsible for rumination, quiets down. The prefrontal cortex lights up, ready for clear thought.

The Future Is Too Noisy for Clarity.

You can't control the future, but you can build strength for it by showing up fully for this second.

Pause Here → Reflection

- How much of your day is spent replaying or preplaying life?

- What sensory cues bring you back into presence fastest?

- What happens in your body when you stop forecasting outcomes?

Try This → Micro Experiment
Set three reminders throughout the day that simply say "Now."
When they appear, pause. Feel your feet, breathe deeply, name five things you can see.
That's your nervous system rebooting to real time.

Quick Wisdom Bite
"The present moment is not a place you visit.
It's the home you forgot you built."

Key	Theme	Represents
	Reflection / Awareness	The inner mirror — for Unrules about mindfulness, self-understanding, and emotional clarity.

UNRULE #33
Failure Isn't Fatal — Stagnation Is

We're taught to fear failure like it's a trapdoor. But most people don't fail because they try — they fail because they freeze.

Psychologists call this "analysis paralysis" — when overthinking drains the energy meant for action.

Failure is friction that shapes form. It polishes purpose.

In business, in love, in art…. motion creates information. Every wrong move teaches you something right for the next step. Every failed attempt generates data your brain files for future precision.
Forward Is a Direction, Not a Speed)

Pause Here → Reflection

- Where have you been holding back in the name of "thinking it through"?

- What could you learn faster by doing instead of planning?

- When was the last time a failure turned into direction?

Try This → Micro Experiment
Take one decision you've been stalling on.
Flip a coin — heads do it, tails release it.
Then observe: which outcome made your body sigh in relief? That's your real answer.

Quick Wisdom Bite
"You can't steer a parked car.
Move first. Adjust later."

Key	Theme	Represents
⚡	Courage / Action	The ignition — for Unrules about momentum, bravery, and saying yes even when it's hard.

UNRULE #34
Ask Better Questions

Your brain is a pattern-seeking machine. It answers whatever question you feed it. Ask, "Why am I stuck?" and it'll find proof of limitation. Ask, "What's possible from here?" and it scans for opportunity.

Coaches, philosophers, and neuroscientists all agree that questions direct attention, and attention directs energy. When you shift the inquiry, you shift the outcome.

The Quality of Your Questions Shapes the Quality of Your Life.

The Quality of Your Questions Shapes the Quality of Your Life
So stop interrogating yourself with blame. Start investigating with curiosity.

Pause Here → Reflection
- What disempowering question do you ask on repeat?

- What would a better question sound like?

- How might your mood change if your self-talk turned investigative instead of critical?

Try This → Micro Experiment
When stuck, replace "Why me?" with "What's this trying to teach me?"
Write both answers side by side.
Notice which one opens more possibilities.

Quick Wisdom Bite
"Better questions build better lives."

Key	Theme	Represents
☾	Reflection / Awareness	The inner mirror — for Unrules about mindfulness, self-understanding, and emotional clarity.

UNRULE #35
Becoming Is Better Than Being

Psychologist Carol Dweck's research on the *growth mindset* revealed something profound: people who see themselves as evolving outperform those who see themselves as fixed. Why? Because they value progress over perfection.

Becoming is messy, beautiful, unfinished. Being is stagnant. When you prioritise evolution, you remove the shame from imperfection — every mistake becomes proof of motion.

You're a Work in Progress — Celebrate That!

You don't have to have it figured out. You just have to be in process. Life's richest moments happen mid-transformation — when you're still stretching, still experimenting, still unsure.
Celebrate that. It means you're alive in the act of creation.

Pause Here → Reflection

- Where do you pressure yourself to "arrive"?

- What would shift if you saw growth as an identity, not a goal?

- How can you measure progress without demanding perfection?

Try This → Micro Experiment

Write a note that says "Under Construction — Please Excuse the Magic."
Stick it somewhere visible.
Every time you feel behind, smile. You're still building.

Quick Wisdom Bite

"You're not incomplete.
You're in motion."

Key	Theme	Represents
🌿	Growth / Renewal	The quiet evolution — for Unrules about healing, learning, and transformation.

UNRULE #36
Connection Is a Daily Practice, Not a Personality Trait

Most people think connection just "happens" — that some are naturally good at it. But neuroscience tells a different story: connection is a skill, not a gift.

Your brain's social circuitry — the prefrontal cortex and mirror neurons — strengthen through use. Every time you show empathy, listen deeply, or share vulnerably, you're literally training your mind to belong.

Belonging Doesn't Happen by Accident.

In a world obsessed with independence, connection feels like rebellion. But our biology hasn't changed — we're wired to co-regulate, to steady our nervous systems through others.

Belonging is a verb. It requires daily action: checking in, reaching out, staying curious.

Pause Here → Reflection

- Who helps regulate your nervous system when life feels chaotic?

- When was the last time you reached out first, without waiting to be asked?

- What daily micro-practices could keep your connections alive?

Try This → Micro Experiment

Send a "thinking of you" message to one person every day for a week.
No agenda. Just presence.
Watch how your sense of connection expands — inward and outward.

Quick Wisdom Bite

"Connection isn't chemistry.
It's repetition."

Key	Theme	Represents
	Reflection / Awareness	The inner mirror — for Unrules about mindfulness, self-understanding, and emotional clarity.

UNRULE #37
Be the Mirror, Not the Mask

Masks are heavy. They protect, but they also suffocate. We wear them to blend in, to impress, to stay safe — but each one distances us from genuine connection.

Psychologist Carl Rogers said the deepest human need is to be fully known and accepted. That can't happen behind armour. When you show up unfiltered, you give others permission to do the same. It's the law of emotional reciprocity: real recognises real.

Authenticity Attracts What Pretence Repels.

Being the mirror means reflecting truth, not performance. When your authenticity meets someone else's, resonance happens — like tuning forks vibrating in sync.

Pause Here → Reflection
- Where are you still performing connection instead of living it?

- What truths about yourself are you afraid to reveal?

- Who makes you feel safe enough to take the mask off?

Try This → Micro Experiment
In your next conversation, share one real thing instead of a polite one. Notice how the energy shifts — authenticity rewires both nervous systems in real time.

Quick Wisdom Bite
"The mask earns approval.
The mirror earns connection."

Key	Theme	Represents
	Growth / Renewal	The quiet evolution — for Unrules about healing, learning, and transformation.

UNRULE #38
Redefine "Your People"

We all crave community, but many of us spend years trying to belong to the wrong rooms.

Fitting in demands conformity; belonging demands truth.
Brené Brown writes, "True belonging doesn't require you to change who you are — it requires you to be who you are." That means some groups, friendships, or even families may no longer fit the version of you that's evolving. That's not rejection. That's resonance doing its work.

Belonging Isn't About Fitting In — It's About Resonance.

When you grow, your frequency shifts. Some connections will vibrate out of tune — let them. New ones will emerge in their place.

Pause Here → Reflection
- Where are you shrinking to stay accepted?

- Who feels like home — and who feels like performance?

- What might "your people" look like in this new chapter of your life?

Try This → Micro Experiment
List three people who energise you and three who drain you.
Spend one more hour this week with the first list — and one less with the second.

That's energetic boundary-setting in action.

Quick Wisdom Bite
"Belonging starts the moment you stop auditioning."

Key	Theme	Represents
	Energy / Passion	The spark of courage, drive, and purpose — for Unrules about daring, doing, and following what lights you up.

UNRULE #39
Practice Generous Listening

Listening is one of the rarest forms of love.

In a world of noise and performance, to truly listen, without waiting for your turn, without planning your reply — is radical empathy. When someone speaks, their brain scans yours for cues of safety. Eye contact, nodding, soft posture, which all signal: "You can keep going."

That exchange releases oxytocin, lowers cortisol, and literally calms both nervous systems. Listening is medicine disguised as attention.

Sometimes Silence Is an Act of Care.

Generous listening isn't about fixing. It's about holding space for another person's unfolding.

Pause Here → Reflection

- How often do you listen to understand versus to respond?

- Who in your life needs less advice and more presence?

- How could you become a calmer mirror for someone else's chaos?

Try This → Micro Experiment

In your next conversation, count to three before replying.
Let the silence breathe.
That's where truth expands.

Quick Wisdom Bite

"Listening is love made audible."

Key	Theme	Represents
	Reflection / Awareness	The inner mirror — for Unrules about mindfulness, self-understanding, and emotional clarity.

UNRULE #40
Say What You Mean, Kindly

There's a myth that honesty and kindness can't coexist. But truth, delivered with care, is the foundation of trust.

Radical candour isn't cruelty, it's clarity with compassion.
When you communicate directly and kindly, you reduce emotional static.

Honesty Is Not a Weapon — It's a Bridge.

Psychologist Marshall Rosenberg called it "nonviolent communication": expressing needs and boundaries without blame or shame.

The result? Relationships that breathe easier.

Pause Here → Reflection

- Where do you sugarcoat truth out of fear of conflict?

- How could honesty become a love language instead of a risk?

- What truth needs saying — softly, but clearly?

Try This → Micro Experiment
Next time you need to give feedback or set a boundary, use this frame:
"When you _____, I feel _____, and I need _____."
Clarity + compassion = connection.

Quick Wisdom Bite
"Truth without tenderness is brutality.
Tenderness without truth is avoidance."

Key	Theme	Represents
	Courage / Action	The ignition — for Unrules about momentum, bravery, and saying yes even when it's hard.

UNRULE #41
Let Go of the Fixer Reflex

You've probably done it — jumped in with a solution before the other person even finished their sentence. It's instinct. We want to stop pain, to tidy mess, to make it right. But often, our urge to fix is really an urge to quiet our own discomfort with someone else's chaos.

Psychologists call this empathetic distress — when we absorb another's struggle so deeply that we rush to end it just to feel relief ourselves. But here's the paradox: fixing often fractures connection. It tells the other person, "Your pain makes me uneasy," instead of, "Your pain can exist here safely."

Support doesn't mean solving.

Carl Rogers described empathy as "entering the private world of another without losing your own." That's the work — being beside, not above. Sometimes the most healing words you can offer are: "That sounds hard. I'm here."

Presence, not prescription, is the medicine.

Pause Here → Reflection

- Who in your life do you try hardest to "fix"?

- What discomfort arises in you when you can't solve someone's pain?

- What might happen if you simply witnessed instead?

Try This → Micro Experiment
When a friend shares something hard, ask:
"Do you want comfort, advice, or just someone to listen?"
Then honour their answer.
It's emotional consent — the highest form of respect.

Quick Wisdom Bite
"Support is not rescue.
It's reverence."

Key	Theme	Represents
	Reflection / Awareness	The inner mirror — for Unrules about mindfulness, self-understanding, and emotional clarity.

UNRULE #42
Forgive Without Forgetting

Forgiveness is a funny one, it isn't about rewriting the past; it's about reclaiming your energy from it.

The myth of "forgive and forget" is just that — a myth. Forgetting erases lessons; forgiveness releases the grip.

Harvard research shows that forgiveness reduces stress hormones, lowers heart rate, and improves sleep. Yet it's rarely immediate. Forgiveness is metabolising the pain — digesting what happened until it no longer defines you.

Think of it like emotional alchemy: you turn resentment into wisdom, hurt into boundaries, chaos into clarity.

Don't pretend the wound never happened; just stop letting it run the show.

Sometimes that means forgiving someone who'll never apologise. Sometimes it means forgiving yourself for what you didn't know then.

Pause Here → Reflection

- What story are you still rehearsing about someone else's mistake?

- What emotion would you free up if you put that narrative down?

- Can forgiveness become an act of power instead of surrender?

Try This → Micro Experiment
Write a letter you'll never send.
Say everything — the rage, the sorrow, the release.
Then burn or tear it up. Let the smoke or scraps carry it off.

Quick Wisdom Bite
"Forgiveness doesn't excuse the past.
It extracts your energy from it."

Key	Theme	Represents
	Growth / Renewal	The quiet evolution — for Unrules about healing, learning, and transformation.

UNRULE #43
Normalize Emotional Check-Ins

Most teams and families run on unspoken emotion. You can feel it before a word is said, it's that tension thick as humidity, joy bright as sunlight.

That's emotional contagion in action: our brains synchronise moods through mirror neurons faster than we can form a sentence.
The problem is, unspoken emotion becomes silent sabotage. It leaks into tone, timing, decisions.

Normalising emotional check-ins — at work, at dinner, in partnerships — is like clearing static from the signal. It lets honesty breathe.

Self-awareness is contagious. Once you start the door is open.

A simple "How's your energy today?" can shift the entire atmosphere. It's not therapy; it's hygiene — keeping the emotional environment clean.

When you name your internal weather, others feel safe to do the same. Vulnerability spreads faster than cynicism when someone goes first.

Pause Here → Reflection

- What emotional climate do you bring into a room?

- Where could a quick "check-in" diffuse misunderstanding before it builds?

- How would your relationships change if truth was a daily ritual?

Try This → Micro Experiment

Start your next meeting, dinner, or morning with a one-word weather report: *Sunny. Foggy. Stormy but clearing.*
No fixing — just noticing.
Watch how honesty becomes contagious.

Quick Wisdom Bite

"Checking in is how we remember we're human."

Key	Theme	Represents
	Reflection / Awareness	The inner mirror — for Unrules about mindfulness, self-understanding, and emotional clarity.

UNRULE #44
Boundaries Build Bridges

Boundaries aren't walls; they're maps. They don't divide love — they define where it can thrive.

Without them, resentment quietly poisons connection. With them, clarity creates ease.

Dr. Brené Brown's research shows that the most compassionate people are also the most boundaried. Why? Because saying "no" with integrity prevents saying "yes" with resentment. Boundaries keep generosity sustainable.

Limits Don't Push People Away — They Show Them Where to Stand.

But boundaries require courage — especially if you grew up believing peace meant pleasing. Setting one can trigger guilt, conflict, or self-doubt. That's your conditioning talking, not your conscience.

A boundary is simply an instruction manual for how to love you well.

Pause Here → Reflection

- Where are you saying yes when your body screams no?

- What boundary could turn irritation into peace?

- How would it feel to see boundaries as an act of respect, not rebellion?

Try This → Micro Experiment

Pick one "leaky" area — time, energy, or attention.
Write one clear line: *"I'm available for X, but not Y."*
Say it calmly once. No apology, no over-explaining.
Notice how relief replaces guilt.

Quick Wisdom Bite

"Boundaries aren't rejection.
They're instruction."

Key	Theme	Represents
⚡	Courage / Action	The ignition — for Unrules about momentum, bravery, and saying yes even when it's hard.

UNRULE #45
Let Joy Be the Glue

We underestimate joy like it's extra credit, you know, something we earn after the real work is done. But joy *is* the work. It's how humans signal safety and belonging to one another.

Neuroscientists have found that shared laughter synchronises breathing, heart rate, and even brainwaves between people. That's why you feel lighter after laughing with someone — your bodies are literally calibrating to harmony.

The real work is letting yourself lap up the 'resilience fuel".

Joy doesn't mean ignoring pain. It's resilience fuel. It says: *We can still find light here.* In long-term relationships, teams, and families, laughter is the emotional equivalent of oil in an engine — reducing friction, keeping things running when life gets rough.

So reclaim your playfulness. Schedule silliness. Be the person who breaks tension with humour, not cynicism. Because joy isn't naive — it's defiant.

Pause Here → Reflection
- Who helps you laugh until your stomach hurts?
- When did you last bring levity to a heavy moment?
- What if joy wasn't the dessert, but the main course?

Try This → Micro Experiment
Create a "joy file": screenshots, notes, ridiculous memories.
Open it whenever the world feels heavy.
Or better yet — share it. Let your joy regulate someone else's nervous system too.

Quick Wisdom Bite
"Joy isn't an afterthought.
It's the connective tissue of life."

Key	Theme	Represents
	Energy / Passion	The spark of courage, drive, and purpose — for Unrules about daring, doing, and following what lights you up.

UNRULE #46
Everything Is Energy (Including You)

You've felt it — the room that hums before a word is spoken. The friend whose presence calms your nervous system without a single sentence. That's energy, not magic.

Quantum physics tells us that everything — from your heartbeat to the chair you're sitting on — vibrates at different frequencies. Matter is just energy slowed down enough to be visible. Your emotions, your thoughts, even your words, all emit measurable frequencies that influence the people and spaces around you.

Stop Trying to Force — Start Learning to Tune.

So when you "tune your energy," you're not just being woo-woo. You're aligning your internal frequency, your physiology and attention, with what you want to amplify. Gratitude raises coherence in your heart's electromagnetic field; resentment distorts it.

Think of yourself as both a transmitter and receiver. The more authentic the signal, the cleaner the resonance.

Pause Here → Reflection
- What energy do you bring into rooms without realising it?
- When do you feel most aligned — calm, curious, or creative?
- What happens in your relationships when you shift that frequency intentionally?

Try This → Micro Experiment
Before your next meeting or conversation, take three deep breaths and silently set an intention:
"May my energy bring clarity and calm."
Then watch how tone, timing, and connection subtly change.

Quick Wisdom Bite
"You're not chasing energy.
You're becoming it."

Key	Theme	Represents
	Chaos / Expansion	The wild unknown — for Unrules about uncertainty, connection, and cosmic perspective.

UNRULE #47
Everything You Do Echoes Somewhere

In 1935, Einstein called it *"spooky action at a distance."* Two particles once connected remain linked, no matter how far apart they travel. Change one, and the other reacts instantly. Quantum entanglement. But here's the twist — you're doing it every day.

Every act of kindness, cruelty, courage, or indifference ripples through invisible networks of influence. You text someone encouragement; they show up braver at work. You snap at your child; they carry that vibration into school. Our fields overlap, constantly entangling and reconfiguring each other.

Entanglement Isn't Just Physics — It's Humanity.

Legacy isn't built later. It's built *now*, in micro-moments of energetic exchange. The smallest gesture can rearrange someone's internal weather.

Pause Here → Reflection

- Who has shaped your life without even knowing it?

- Where might your actions be echoing further than you can see?

- What legacy are you transmitting right now — consciously or unconsciously?

Try This → Micro Experiment

Pick one day to become acutely aware of your ripple.
Smile at the stranger. Compliment the colleague.
Notice how one act of generosity alters the tone of your entire environment.

Quick Wisdom Bite

"Entanglement means you never move alone."

Key	Theme	Represents
■	Chaos / Expansion	The wild unknown — for Unrules about uncertainty, connection, and cosmic perspective.

UNRULE #48
Attention Is Creation

In quantum mechanics, the *observer effect* states that the very act of watching changes the behaviour of what's being observed. A particle is both wave and solid until someone looks — then, it becomes one or the other.

Sound familiar? You live this every day.

What you focus on crystallises. What you ignore dissolves. Energy follows attention — and attention, biologically speaking, is the brain's way of saying, "This matters."

What You Observe Expands.

When you fixate on lack, your brain filters reality through scarcity. When you attune to potential, your neural pathways literally start scanning for it. The external shifts because your internal lens does. This isn't toxic positivity. It's neuroplasticity — your brain responding to intention.

Pause Here → Reflection

- What outcomes have you accidentally reinforced by over-focusing on fear?

- Where does your attention need pruning or redirection?

- How might observing possibility change your perception of self?

Try This → Micro Experiment

Set a timer every few hours. When it rings, ask:
"What am I noticing right now?"
Then choose one micro-shift — gratitude, curiosity, awe.
Over time, those moments compound into an upgraded reality.

Quick Wisdom Bite

"Reality rearranges itself around what you see."

Key	Theme	Represents
	Reflection / Awareness	The inner mirror — for Unrules about mindfulness, self-understanding, and emotional clarity.

UNRULE #49
Live as the Experiment, Not the Outcome

Particles in a quantum field exist as waves of probability until measured. In human terms: your potential collapses only when you stop imagining new possibilities.

We've been trained to crave closure — to tidy up life's equations with clear outcomes and predictable patterns. But creativity, growth, and meaning live in the unknown — in the wave, not the particle.

Stay in the Quantum State of Becoming.

When you stop demanding certainty, you make space for emergence. That's where intuition thrives, innovation happens, and identity evolves. You are a living experiment — constantly collapsing new realities with every choice you make.
Freedom isn't found in knowing; it's found in staying curious.

Pause Here → Reflection

- What part of your life are you trying too hard to define?

- How would you live differently if you saw yourself as "in progress," not incomplete?

- Where might uncertainty actually be your ally?

Try This → Micro Experiment

Replace one daily decision with an experiment.
"What if I try this instead?"
Notice how curiosity quiets anxiety — that's your brain switching from threat to possibility mode.

Quick Wisdom Bite

"You are both the scientist and the spark."

Key	Theme	Represents
🌱	Growth / Renewal	The quiet evolution — for Unrules about healing, learning, and transformation.

UNRULE #50
You Are Part of the Field

Quantum theory ends where spirituality begins: everything is connected through an unseen field of energy. Every thought, choice, and emotion ripples through that field — altering not just your trajectory, but the collective one.

Purpose isn't a singular destination. It's how you *interact* with the field — how your presence shapes the whole.

When you create, heal, listen, or love, you contribute to coherence. When you isolate, numb, or withhold, the field reflects that too. It's never judgment — just resonance.

Purpose Is Participation, Not Perfection.

So, purpose isn't about being grand or flawless. It's about showing up, again and again, as a conscious participant in the cosmic experiment of being human.

Pause Here → Reflection

- How does your daily energy influence the collective field you move through?

- What does contribution look like for you — right now, not someday?

- Can you feel the difference between striving for perfection and offering presence?

Try This → Micro Experiment

Each morning, ask:
"How can I add harmony to the field today?"
Then do one small act that brings coherence — to your home, team, or inner state.

Quick Wisdom Bite

"Purpose isn't something you find.
It's something you feed."

Key	Theme	Represents
■	Chaos / Expansion	The wild unknown — for Unrules about uncertainty, connection, and cosmic perspective.

UNRULE #51
Make Peace with Impermanence

Everything you love — every place, every person, every version of you — will change, fade, or vanish. That's not tragedy; that's physics. Entropy is the universe's heartbeat. The same law that pulls stars apart also fuels evolution.

Impermanence terrifies us because it exposes our lack of control. Yet when you accept it, life becomes painfully, beautifully vivid.

The Japanese call it *mono no aware* — the bittersweet awareness of transience. The flower's beauty *because* it wilts. The laughter's glow *because* it ends.

Nothing Lasts and That's the Point.

You can't hold time. But you can hold presence.
And in that moment of awareness, right here, right now, you realise nothing's slipping away. It's just changing form.

Pause Here → Reflection
- What have you been clinging to out of fear of loss?

- How would you live differently if you saw endings as transformations?

- Can impermanence become a reason to love more fiercely?

Try This → Micro Experiment
Next time something ends — a project, a season, a chapter — resist the urge to replace it. Sit in the quiet aftermath.
Notice what emerges in the space left behind.

Quick Wisdom Bite
"Everything ends. That's what makes it worth living."

Key	Theme	Represents
🌱	Growth / Renewal	The quiet evolution — for Unrules about healing, learning, and transformation.

UNRULE #52
Curiosity Is the Antidote to Fear

Fear tightens, curiosity expands.

When you're afraid, your brain collapses possibility into threat. But when you ask a question, your neural circuits shift — dopamine, oxytocin, and prefrontal engagement turn panic into problem-solving. This is neurobiology's version of courage.

Curiosity doesn't erase fear; it metabolises it.

Curiosity says, *"I see you — now what can I learn from this?"*

Socrates called wisdom "the recognition of ignorance." Every question loosens fear's grip because it reminds you that mystery isn't an enemy — it's an invitation.

Pause Here → Reflection

- What situation are you meeting with fear instead of curiosity?

- How could one better question change your perspective today?

- Where might wonder be braver than certainty?

Try This → Micro Experiment
Write down one recurring worry.
Underneath it, list three curious questions that start with "What if…" or "How might…"
Watch how your nervous system softens the moment inquiry replaces control.

Quick Wisdom Bite
"Fear freezes. Curiosity frees."

Key	Theme	Represents
⚡	Courage / Action	The ignition — for Unrules about momentum, bravery, and saying yes even when it's hard.

UNRULE #53
Fall in Love with Ordinary Days

We keep chasing "more", more achievement, more awe, more noise. Yet the deepest moments of fulfilment often happen in the spaces in between.

Psychologist Mihaly Csikszentmihalyi called it *flow*: full immersion in something simple — chopping vegetables, fixing a bike, walking under late light. Your brain hums in quiet coherence.

The ordinary is where your nervous system resets. It's where awe learns to whisper.

Often meaning hides in plain sight.

You don't need to reinvent your life to feel alive. You just need to notice it.

Pause Here → Reflection
- When was the last time you felt quietly content?

- What ordinary rituals already anchor your joy?

- How can you turn daily repetition into devotion?

Try This → Micro Experiment
For one week, photograph one "mundane miracle" a day — light on your coffee cup, laughter at the sink, a child's hand on yours. Collect them. That's your real highlight reel.

Quick Wisdom Bite
"The extraordinary is just the ordinary, seen fully."

Key	Theme	Represents
	Growth / Renewal	The quiet evolution — for Unrules about healing, learning, and transformation.

UNRULE #54
Don't Outsource Your Worth

We live in a culture addicted to comparison — followers, likes, promotions, perfection. The dopamine hit of validation has rewired entire generations. But neuroscience is clear: external reward systems hijack intrinsic motivation, leaving emptiness where purpose should be.

You weren't built to be measured; you were built to express. Self-worth is reclaimed when you stop outsourcing value to algorithms or applause and return it to action, creation, and alignment.

The metrics were never meant to be yours.

Nietzsche warned of *herd morality* — losing individuality in the crowd's opinion. Freedom begins when you stop auditioning for approval you no longer need.

Pause Here → Reflection

- Where are you performing instead of expressing?

- What external scorecard still defines your self-worth?

- What would "enough" look like if no one else was watching?

Try This → Micro Experiment
Next time you catch yourself checking for feedback — social, emotional, professional — pause.
Ask: "If this mattered only to me, would I still do it?"
If yes, that's alignment.

Quick Wisdom Bite
"Validation fades. Value remains."

Key	Theme	Represents
	Energy / Passion	The spark of courage, drive, and purpose — for Unrules about daring, doing, and following what lights you up.

UNRULE #55
Let Grief Teach You How to Love

Grief isn't a malfunction. It's the body's proof of attachment — love looking for somewhere to go.

Neuroscience shows grief lights up the same neural pathways as physical pain. That ache in your chest is your nervous system re-mapping connection.

But grief is also generative. Over time, the brain rewires. The love doesn't vanish; it transforms into memory, legacy, compassion. You begin to live with — not without — what's gone.

Loss Is the Proof That You Lived.

Philosopher Alain de Botton wrote, "We only grieve because we have loved well."
That's the deal. Love deeply, lose deeply. But also live more vividly because of it.

Pause Here → Reflection
- What or who are you learning to live with, not without?

- How can grief become a teacher, not a thief?

- What would it mean to let sorrow soften you, not shrink you?

Try This → Micro Experiment
Light a candle tonight.
As it burns, whisper one truth you learned from the person or thing you lost.
That's love, still working through you.

Quick Wisdom Bite
"Grief is love, rearranged."

Key	Theme	Represents
	Growth / Renewal	The quiet evolution — for Unrules about healing, learning, and transformation.

UNRULE #56
Build a Life That Fits Your Nervous System

You can chase goals, wealth, and status — but if your nervous system is constantly in fight-or-flight, you're building a cage, not a life.

The vagus nerve — your body's "safety switch" — doesn't care about your CV. It only responds to regulation: breath, connection, environment, rest. Chronic stress keeps it constricted; calm expands it, restoring clarity, creativity, and joy.

Success Without Safety Isn't Success.

So maybe the new success metric isn't hustle — it's harmony., because a regulated nervous system is the foundation of authentic performance.

Pause Here → Reflection.
- What achievements still left you anxious or numb?

- How does your body tell you when it feels safe — or not?

- What would you redesign if your nervous system was the CEO?

Try This → Micro Experiment
Before major tasks, inhale deeply for four counts, exhale for six.
That longer exhale tells your body, *You're safe here.*
Then proceed — not from adrenaline, but from alignment.

Quick Wisdom Bite
"Peace is productivity's missing variable."

Key	Theme	Represents
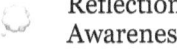	Reflection / Awareness	The inner mirror — for Unrules about mindfulness, self-understanding, and emotional clarity.

UNRULE #57
Legacy Is How You Make People Feel

When people remember you, they'll forget most of your achievements. But they'll never forget how they felt in your presence.

That's the legacy that lasts — emotional resonance.
Every interaction leaves an imprint on another person's nervous system. The calmer, kinder, or more curious you are, the safer others feel — and the more likely they are to pay that safety forward.

Your Energy Outlives You.

It's emotional ripple physics. Your field lives on in others.

Pause Here → Reflection

- What emotional footprint do you leave behind?

- Who made you feel safe enough to grow — and have you thanked them?

- How could you multiply that feeling in others today?

Try This → Micro Experiment
Text someone who once made you feel seen.
Tell them specifically what it meant.
That single message might shift their entire day — or life.

Quick Wisdom Bite
"You won't be remembered for what you had.
You'll be remembered for how you held people."

Key	Theme	Represents
	Chaos / Expansion	The wild unknown — for Unrules about uncertainty, connection, and cosmic perspective.

UNRULE #58
Rest Is a Rebellion

We glorify burnout and call it drive. But rest isn't laziness — it's resistance.

In a system built to measure human worth by output, pausing becomes a radical act of reclamation.

Your brain consolidates learning during rest. Your heart recalibrates coherence. Your spirit refills its creative reservoir. Even the universe works in cycles — inhale and exhale, light and dark, expansion and collapse.

Stillness Is the Antidote to the Machine.

So rest, unapologetically. The world won't end if you nap. But you might if you don't.

Pause Here → Reflection
- When did you last stop without guilt?

- What beliefs still make rest feel "unearned"?

- How would your days change if you saw rest as fuel, not failure?

Try This → Micro Experiment
Schedule rest like a meeting.
Protect it with the same ferocity you give deadlines.
When you rest consciously, you reset creatively.

Quick Wisdom Bite
"Rest isn't quitting. It's reclaiming."

Key	Theme	Represents
	Growth / Renewal	The quiet evolution — for Unrules about healing, learning, and transformation.

UNRULE #59
Stop Measuring, Start Experiencing

We've turned everything into a scoreboard — steps, followers, revenue, likes. But you can't quantify awe, intimacy, or transcendence. Data gives feedback, not meaning.

Psychologist Daniel Kahneman called it the "experiencing self" versus the "remembering self." One lives; the other evaluates.
When you live to measure, you abandon the moment for its potential story.

Metrics Can't Capture Magic.

Presence isn't productive. It's participatory.

Stop counting; start feeling.

Pause Here → Reflection

- Where have you replaced experience with evidence?

- What's one area of your life that's over-measured but under-lived?

- How might unquantified joy feel?

Try This → Micro Experiment

Go one full day without tracking anything — no numbers, no metrics, no proof.
Just *be*.
Notice how your senses wake up.

Quick Wisdom Bite

"The unmeasured life is where wonder lives."

Key	Theme	Represents
	Reflection / Awareness	The inner mirror — for Unrules about mindfulness, self-understanding, and emotional clarity.

UNRULE #60
Leave Light Everywhere You Go

If every particle is connected, every smile is a signal.
Kindness shifts biochemistry — oxytocin in giver and receiver, serotonin for mood, dopamine for connection. It's biology's feedback loop for good.

Every act of grace adds coherence to the collective field. That's not metaphor — it's measurable energy. In physics, coherence creates stability. In humanity, it creates hope.

Kindness Is Quantum.

Your task isn't to save the world. It's to keep adding light until the dark can't hold.

Pause Here → Reflection
- How can you add light to one life today — including your own?

- What happens when you choose compassion before reaction?

- What legacy of light do you want to leave?

Try This → Micro Experiment
End every day by asking:
"Did I leave more light than I found?"
If not, tomorrow's another chance.

Quick Wisdom Bite
"Kindness is the physics of the soul."

Key	Theme	Represents
	Energy / Passion	The spark of courage, drive, and purpose — for Unrules about daring, doing, and following what lights you up.

UNRULE #61
Let the Universe Edit You

You've rewritten your résumé. Your relationships. Your routines. But what about your story?

Every few years, life hands you an unexpected red pen — illness, heartbreak, success, surprise. You can fight the edits or collaborate with them.
Because sometimes, the universe doesn't cross things out to punish you. It edits to refine the plot.

Growth Means Rewriting Yourself Again and Again.

Quantum theory says particles flicker between possibilities until observed. Likewise, you're never finished. Every experience collapses one version of you so another can emerge. It's not destruction — it's evolution through draft.

Perfection was never the goal. Participation was.

Pause Here → Reflection

- What chapter of your story are you still trying to write in permanent ink?

- Which "mistakes" might actually be creative rewrites?

- What if becoming your best self meant deleting parts that no longer fit?

Try This → Micro Experiment

Print a page of your own old writing — a journal entry, a social post, even a list. Edit it. Remove words that no longer sound like you. That's your metaphor: you get to re-author yourself at will.

Quick Wisdom Bite

"Reinvention isn't rebellion. It's revision."

Key	Theme	Represents
	Growth / Renewal	The quiet evolution — for Unrules about healing, learning, and transformation.

UNRULE #62
Stop Worshipping Balance — Seek Harmony Instead

"Work-life balance" sounds noble, but it's a myth built for spreadsheets.

Balance implies stasis, as if your entire existence should sit evenly on a scale. But real life moves — more jazz than metronome. Harmony, on the other hand, allows tension. In music, dissonance resolves into beauty. You don't need equal parts of everything — just intentional flow.

ated *Life Isn't Scales; It's a Symphony.*

Neuroscience shows your brain doesn't multitask; it oscillates. Focus deeply, then rest completely. That rhythm creates creativity and longevity.

Harmony doesn't demand that you juggle perfectly. It asks that you listen.

Pause Here → Reflection

- What are you forcing to "balance" that might simply need rhythm?

- How do your energy cycles actually sound — sharp, soft, or silent?

- Could harmony, not equality, be your new measure of success?

Try This → Micro Experiment
Design your next week like a song.
What's your verse (work), your chorus (connection), your rest (pause)?
Play it out loud — imperfections included.

Quick Wisdom Bite
"Stop chasing balance. Conduct harmony."

Key	Theme	Represents
	Energy / Passion	The spark of courage, drive, and purpose — for Unrules about daring, doing, and following what lights you up.

UNRULE #63
The Opposite of Control Is Trust

Control feels safe. It gives the illusion of certainty — the neat boxes, the scheduled future. But control is a nervous system strategy, not a life philosophy.

The irony? The more you tighten, the more the universe resists. Chaos theory proves that small variables create massive changes. Trust doesn't mean giving up; it means dancing with variables that aren't yours to hold.

Faith Is Just Physics You Haven't Understood Yet.

You can't dominate the ocean. You surf it. You can't micromanage destiny. You meet it halfway.

Pause Here → Reflection

- What's one part of life you're strangling into stillness?

- How would it feel to replace control with collaboration?

- Where is the tide already trying to help you move forward?

Try This → Micro Experiment

Take one decision off autopilot today. Flip a coin, go with instinct, or let someone else choose the restaurant.
Notice how surrender makes space for surprise.

Quick Wisdom Bite

"Trust isn't passive. It's participatory surrender."

Key	Theme	Represents
■	Chaos / Expansion	The wild unknown — for Unrules about uncertainty, connection, and cosmic perspective.

UNRULE #64
Create Beauty Even When It Hurts

When life breaks you open, make something from the pieces. That's not romanticism; it's survival.

Artists, poets, scientists — all translate pain into pattern. Neuroscience shows that creating after trauma activates the brain's reward and empathy networks. Beauty is the nervous system's way of re-balancing itself.

Don't wait until the storm clears to create. Paint with the rain still falling.

Art Is How the Soul Exhales.

Every scar, every heartbreak, every grief is a pigment. Mix them honestly, and you'll find meaning where despair once lived.

Pause Here → Reflection
- What beauty has pain been quietly offering you?

- Which story are you finally ready to translate into art — in any form?

- How could creating become your way of healing?

Try This → Micro Experiment
Pick one emotion that scares you. Write, draw, move, or speak it. Don't aim for pretty — aim for truth.

Quick Wisdom Bite
"Art alchemises pain into pattern."

Key	Theme	Represents
	Growth / Renewal	The quiet evolution — for Unrules about healing, learning, and transformation.

UNRULE #65
The Universe Responds to Participation, Not Perfection

You keep waiting until you're ready. But readiness is a mirage that disappears as you approach. The universe doesn't reward perfection; it multiplies momentum.

Quantum theory calls it "collapse of the wave function." Potential becomes reality only when energy interacts. Life works the same way — nothing happens until you step in.

Show Up Messy — The Field Doesn't Care About Polish.

Perfection isolates. Participation connects.
The field responds to engagement. Not someday. Today.

Pause Here → Reflection

- Where are you hiding behind preparation?

- What unfinished dream could you energise simply by showing up?

- What if progress, not polish, is what the field responds to?

Try This → Micro Experiment

Start something deliberately imperfect — a rough draft, an awkward conversation, a shaky idea.
Movement is the magic.

Quick Wisdom Bite

"The universe can't amplify silence."

Key	Theme	Represents
⚡	Courage / Action	The ignition — for Unrules about momentum, bravery, and saying yes even when it's hard.

UNRULE #66
You Are the Continuum

You're not a moment; you're a motion. Every thought, every choice, every act of care contributes to a continuum that began long before you and will outlive your name.

Legacy isn't built in retirement speeches. It's built in daily ripples.

The neuroscientist V.S. Ramachandran once wrote that mirror neurons make us natural mimics — we echo what we witness. That's how legacies spread: not through monuments, but through mannerisms, through kindness, through presence.

Legacy Isn't Later — It's Now.

You are someone's echo. You will become someone's imprint. That is immortality enough.

Pause Here → Reflection

- What behaviours of others live unconsciously in you?

- How might your actions ripple into lives you'll never meet?

- What small continuity of goodness could you choose today?

Try This → Micro Experiment
Do one generous act and tell no one.
Legacy isn't what's seen — it's what's sustained.

Quick Wisdom Bite
"You're not a story. You're a sequence."

Key	Theme	Represents
	Energy / Passion	The spark of courage, drive, and purpose — for Unrules about daring, doing, and following what lights you up.

UNRULE #67
THE INVITATION
Your Turn to Break the Rules

There's no final page here. Only you, the reader, standing where ink meets possibility.

Everything you've read — the science, the philosophy, the chaos and the tenderness has been a rehearsal. A set of experiments for your own becoming. The rest of this book is unwritten, because it's now happening through you.

Take what resonates, remix what doesn't. Turn Unrules into rituals, or let them crumble into compost for your next version.

That's the whole point.

Because this isn't a book about following. It's a book about remembering that you're already the author.

The Experiment Continues — in You.

So go create. Break your own patterns. Add light, add laughter, add one small tremor of change.

The field is waiting for your signal.

Pause Here → Reflection

- What Unrule will you rewrite first?

- What story are you ready to tell with your own frequency?

- What if the "next" isn't out there — but right here, in how you live?

Quick Wisdom Bite

"The rules were never real. The becoming always was."

THE FINAL WORD

You've made it here, to this quiet place at the back of the book.
It's still here. You can almost hear your own thoughts again.
That voice in your head, the one reading these words —
who is that, anyway?
Maybe you underlined a few things.
Maybe you argued with a few Unrules.
Maybe you just let them wash over you with your morning coffee.
It doesn't matter.
You've been in conversation with yourself — and that's the real work.
The point of all this isn't to arrive somewhere polished or certain.
It's to stay awake.
To keep noticing.
To live like your life is a studio, not a museum.
Every Unrule was an invitation to remember:
You are simply becoming, over and over again.
So if you take nothing else from these pages, take this:
Your life is not a problem to be solved.
There is no finish line to success.
It's a story to be lived, fully, fiercely, and maybe a little out of bounds.
Keep burning the old scripts.
Keep writing new ones.
Keep laughing in the middle of it all, because the real magic isn't in the rule you break, it's in the freedom you discover after you do.

NOTES & REFERENCES

The following thinkers, scientists, and storytellers helped shape the ideas explored throughout What The Hell Next!? — from the spark of chaos to the quiet art of becoming.

Their work sits at the intersection of science, philosophy, and soul — the same space these 66 Unrules were born from.

Psychology & Neuroscience
- Brown, B. (2012). *Daring Greatly*. Gotham Books.
- Dweck, C. (2006). Mindset: The New Psychology of Success. Random House.
- Kahneman, D. (2011). *Thinking, Fast and Slow*. Farrar, Straus and Giroux.
- Rogers, C. (1961). *On Becoming a Person*. Houghton Mifflin.
- Merzenich, M. (2013). Soft-Wired: How the New Science of Brain Plasticity Can Change Your Life. Parnassus.
- Yalom, I. (1980). Existential Psychotherapy. Basic Books.
- Davidson, R. J. & Begley, S. (2012). *The Emotional Life of Your Brain*. Hudson Street Press.
- Kabat-Zinn, J. (1990). *Full Catastrophe Living*. Delacorte.
- Siegel, D. (2007). *The Mindful Brain*. Norton.
- Goleman, D. (1995). *Emotional Intelligence*. Bantam.
- Black, A. et al. (2010). Authenticity and Well-Being During Life Transitions. *Journal of Positive Psychology*.

Philosophy & Thought
- Nietzsche, F. (1883). *Thus Spoke Zarathustra*.
- Kierkegaard, S. (1843). *Fear and Trembling*.
- Socrates (via Plato, 360 BCE). *The Dialogues*.
- Confucius (551–479 BCE). *The Analects*.

- Lao Tzu (6th century BCE). *Tao Te Ching*.
- Tolle, E. (1999). *The Power of Now*. New World Library.
- Frankl, V. (1946). Man's Search for Meaning. Beacon Press.
- de Beauvoir, S. (1949). *The Second Sex*.
- Camus, A. (1942). *The Myth of Sisyphus*.
- Arendt, H. (1958). *The Human Condition*.
- Watts, A. (1951). The Wisdom of Insecurity. Pantheon.

Behavioural Science & Sociology
- Lorenz, E. (1963). Deterministic Nonperiodic Flow. *Journal of the Atmospheric Sciences, 20*(2), 130–141.
- Putnam, R. (2000). Bowling Alone: The Collapse and Revival of American Community. Simon & Schuster.
- Duckworth, A. (2016). Grit: The Power of Passion and Perseverance. Scribner.
- Duhigg, C. (2012). *The Power of Habit*. Random House.
- Seligman, M. (2011). Flourish: A Visionary New Understanding of Happiness and Well-Being. Atria Books.
- Deci, E. & Ryan, R. (2000). Self-Determination Theory. *Psychological Inquiry*.

Inspiration & Modern Voices
- Clear, J. (2018). *Atomic Habits*. Avery.
- Dyer, W. (1976). Your Erroneous Zones. Warner Books.
- Brown, S. (2009). Play: How It Shapes the Brain, Opens the Imagination, and Invigorates the Soul. Avery.
- Robbins, M. (2017). *The 5 Second Rule*. Savio Republic.
- Grant, A. (2021). *Think Again*. Viking.
- Maté, G. (2022). *The Myth of Normal*. Knopf.
- Levine, P. (1997). Waking the Tiger: Healing Trauma. North Atlantic Books.

- Dispenza, J. (2012). Breaking the Habit of Being Yourself. Hay House.
- van der Kolk, B. (2014). *The Body Keeps the Score*. Penguin.
- Sharma, R. (2003). The Monk Who Sold His Ferrari. HarperCollins.
- Roddick, A. (1991). *Business as Unusual*. Thorsons.

Quantum, Chaos & Systems Thinking
- Lorenz, E. (1963). *The Essence of Chaos*. University of Washington Press.
- Capra, F. (1975). *The Tao of Physics*. Shambhala.
- Prigogine, I. & Stengers, I. (1984). *Order Out of Chaos*. Bantam.
- Bohm, D. (1980). Wholeness and the Implicate Order. Routledge.
- Heisenberg, W. (1958). *Physics and Philosophy*. Harper.
- Wheeler, J. A. (1990). Information, Physics, Quantum: The Search for Links. Proceedings of the 3rd International Symposium on the Foundations of Quantum Mechanics.
- Gleick, J. (1987). Chaos: Making a New Science. Penguin.
- Penrose, R. (1989). *The Emperor's New Mind*. Oxford University Press.

Leadership, Change & Human Potential
- Kotter, J. (1996). *Leading Change*. Harvard Business Review Press.
- Senge, P. (1990). *The Fifth Discipline*. Doubleday.
- Wheatley, M. (2006). Leadership and the New Science. Berrett-Koehler.
- Csikszentmihalyi, M. (1990). Flow: The Psychology of Optimal Experience. Harper Perennial.

- Pink, D. (2009). Drive: The Surprising Truth About What Motivates Us. Riverhead Books.

- Boyatzis, R. & McKee, A. (2005). *Resonant Leadership*. Harvard Business Press.
- Brown, B. (2018). *Dare to Lead*. Random House.

Additional Research & Case Studies
- ACTIVE Study Group (2006). Advanced Cognitive Training for Independent and Vital Elderly. *JAMA, 296*(23).
- Australian Institute of Health and Welfare (2022). *Social Isolation and Wellbeing*.
- UCLA Loneliness Study (2018). Proceedings of the National Academy of Sciences.
- Harvard Study of Adult Development (2015). *Journal of Happiness Studies*.
- Carnegie Mellon University (2003). Optimism and Immune Function. *Health Psychology, 22*(3).
- Journal of Applied Positive Psychology (2021). Mindset Interventions in Adult Learning.
- Science of People (2025). Existential Crises and Adult Reinvention Study.
- AIHW (2024). Mental Health and Connection in Midlife Adults: Insights for Wellbeing.

www.ingramcontent.com/pod-product-compliance
Lightning Source LLC
Chambersburg PA
CBHW022016290426
44109CB00015B/1193